Swallo the Sun
and Other Poems

Written by Samantha Montgomerie
Illustrated by Felishia Henditirto, Komal Pahwa
and Emily Paik

Collins

Swallowing the Sun

Have you seen how the sea
swallows the sun?

The sea licks its lips with a lazy slap,
watching the sun with its
slow glide, low ride,
seabound slide.

Then —

Snap!

The glare melts
to apricot-gold,
as a pearly satin unfolds on
glassy waters.

A last gasp of amber light
sends glistening candyfloss into the sky.

Shadow winged birds call
and wink.

The birds freeze there ...
mid-air,
as the flare
starts to sink.

The sea's full stomach
grumbles and groans,
foamy tips washing
in lullaby tones.

Glisten and slap –
the sea sighs and laps,
dozing on its sun feast as
the world turns black.

Beware

Watch out raindrops!
You'd better beware.
Jack Frost is out there,
chilling the air.

His icy breath whistling
there in the sky.
He wants to snatch you
as you drift on by.

Feel the rawness on the breeze,
waiting to catch you
and make you freeze.

Beware, beware,
Jack Frost is there –
making bullets of hail
that fall like spears.

Catch a Wave!

Catch a wave, catch it,
ride it in.
Slice through the water
like a shark's slick fin.

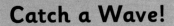

Whistle along,
let your cares drift out to sea ...
as you
          water-fly and
                        foam-ride

merrily.

Wet-Wobble Dog Shake

Tearing after gulls,
catching washed-up balls,

yip and yap,
tearing back ...

Watch out! Beware!
A wet-wobble dog shake
is watering the air!

The High Dive

Clutching the rail, fear setting in —
one step, catch my breath,
a quivering chin.

Freeze.

Water far below,
feet shuffle slow.

Then —

Jump!

Whistling through air,
whistling past fear,
whistling fun, airy run.

Then –

Splash!

Watery bubbles,
spine-tingling shivers.

Quick! Run!

I tear on up
to catch
some high-diving fun!

Rain Song

There's a rain song on my roof.
Listen – can you hear?
A tip-tip-tap, a watery splash,
like a silver bell is near.

Could the drum roll have begun?
There's water pounding down,
with a thundering smash, a watery crash,
washing us with sound.

Listen, listen – hear that there?
The wind is whistling without a care!

Catch the beat, hear the thrum.
A watery rain song is lots of fun!

Poetry prompts

Can you write a poem about one of these pictures?

Writing tips for poetry

- Read it out — hear what it sounds like.
- Could you find a word that sounds better?
- Do your words help the reader hear, feel and see the scene?

Five facts on Jack Frost

The legend began in Viking tales.

Jack Frost means "Icicle Frost" in Norse.

He was the son of the Norse wind god.

He made things freeze.

He painted frosty patterns on windows.

Water poems

Beware

Swallowing the Sun

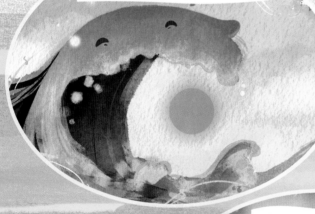

Rain Song

Catch a Wave!

Wet-Wobble
Dog Shake

The High Dive

31

❧ Review: After reading ❧

Use your assessment from hearing the children read to choose any GPCs, words or tricky words that need additional practice.

Read 1: Decoding

- Ask the children to read these words. Ask them to find the /air/ sounds and the /ch/ sounds. Encourage them to point to the letters that make up these sounds.

  there   glare   tearing   flare   snatch   catch   pictures

- Challenge the children to read pages 2 and 3 fluently. Say: Can you sound out the words in your head silently, before reading them aloud? Discuss the meaning of **swallows** in the context of the sun setting over the sea.

- Bonus content: Ask the children to read page 26. Focus on the meaning of **scene** in the context of a poem. Pick a scene from pages 24 and 25 and ask: How might a poet **help the reader hear, feel and see** it?

Read 2: Prosody

- Challenge the children to read pages 14 and 15 expressively, to build an atmosphere of excitement.

  o Discuss the best tone for the opening two lines. (e.g. *encouraging, excited*) Ask: How might your tone change for page 15? (e.g. *a light-hearted, fun-sounding tone*)

  o Discuss how the onomatopoeic words can be brought alive. (e.g. *slice – a short sharp tone;* **Whistle** *– a long airy tone*)

- Bonus content: Ask the children to read pages 28 and 29 in the voice of a documentary narrator. To capture the listeners' respect and attention, can they sound authoritative and interested?

Read 3: Comprehension

- Ask the children which poem they like most and why. Encourage them to talk about anything similar that they have seen, heard or felt.

- On page 5, discuss what colours are meant by **amber** and **candyfloss**. Talk about how metaphors (comparing two things that are the same in a particular way) bring the scenes in the poems alive.

- Turn to pages 30 and 31 and recall each poem. Ask: Can you remember any sights, sounds or feelings from this poem? Which poem do you remember best? Why do you think this is?